Fimark's Family Reunion
A Reunion Planning Guide Workbook & Keepsake

"Hand n Hand"

This Book Belongs To: _____

Fimark's Family Reunion Planner
A Family Reunion Planning Guide Workbook and Keepsake

Copyright © 2011 Mark A. Askew/Fimark.net (Financial Marketing Network, Inc.) All Rights Reserved.
FIRST EDITION, 2011

All rights reserved under international and Pan-American Copyright Conventions. No part of this book may be reproduced in any form or by any electronic or mechanical means, including information storage and retrieval systems, without permission in writing by the publisher, except by reviewers or catalogues not limited to online for purpose of promotion.

Published by CreateSpace at CreateSpace.com and distributed by Amazon.com and associated distribution channels. Materials such as images contained are copyright to Mark Askew, Fimark.net, Fimark Home Online 2011 of Baltimore, Maryland. Images used retain original copyright and maintain ownership. Other images are copyright of the Author and are also subject to the same copyright restrictions as text.

Fimark.net - Fimark Home Online – Fimark Event Planners
http://family-reunion-planner.fimark.net

Askew, M. A., 2011

ISBN-13: 978-1461124238
ISBN-10: 1461124239
Fimark's Family Reunion Planner
A Family Reunion Planning Guide Workbook and Keepsake

Printed In North America

This Edition

Black and White Paperback: Grey scale digital graphic renderings.

Other Editions

Full Color Hard Cover: Full color digital graphic renderings.
Black and White Hard Cover: scale digital graphic renderings.
eBook: Color Grey scale digital graphic renderings.

First Edition Bound: Grey scale digital graphic renderings.

Contents:

- Event Details — Page 3
- Forward — Page 4
- Acknowledgements — Page 5
- Proclamations and Observances — Page 6
- Tutorial — Page 7
- Reunion Planning For Coordinators — Page 10
- Reunion Planning For Committees — Page 12
- Advanced Timeline Planner — Page 15
- Reunion Planning Checklist — Page 17
- Themes — Page 19
- Cruise - Family Reunion — Page 20
- Family Culture Fest — Page 31
- Genealogy & Homestead Tour — Page 34
- Living Legends Ball — Page 36
- Journal- My Reunion Journal — Page 38
- Committees Lists — Page 68
- Dept. Assignments Worksheets — Page 69
- Follow-up Notes — Page 70
- Event Planner Worksheet — Page 73
- Site Location Sheet — Page 74
- Scheduling Worksheet — Page 75
- Consideration Element — Page 76
- Activities Worksheet — Page 78
- Possible Locations/Activities — Page 79
- Games — Page 80
- Needs List — Page 82
- Hotel Accommodations Checklist — Page 83
- Hotel Booking Cost Comparison — Page 84
- Meals/Menu — Page 85
- Agenda for Lunch/Dinner Program — Page 86
- My Reunion Recipes — Page 90
- Certificates — Page 100
- Music Selection Sheet — Page 101
- Directions/Map — Page 102
- Fund Raiser Ideas — Page 103
- Reunion Evaluation Sheet — Page 104
- Next Reunion event Plans — Page 105
- Pedigree — Page 106
- Family Group Worksheet — Page 108
- Cemetery transcription form — Page 110
- Heirloom possession verification — Page 111
- Military records research checklist — Page 112
- Ancestral research work sheet — Page 114
- Survey Form Letter — Page 117
- Luncheon/Dinner Program — Page 119
- Itinerary — Page 120
- Invitational Letter — Page 122
- Software Evaluation Features — Page 124
- References — Page 125
- Resources — Page 126
- Index — Page 127

Event Details

Theme: _____

Date(s): _____

Slogan: _____

Location: _____

Chairperson: _____

Details:

_____

_____

_____

_____

Contacts:

_____ _____

_____ _____

"Though thousands of miles apart, her children once scattered across a vast country set this date in stone and mapped out a course and one by one each daughter and son made a journey home.
They made a journey home."

Excerpts from "Finding Our Way Back Home"
By Mark Askew

Forward

Congratulations on your upcoming family reunion event. You are about to embark on an ever growing, fascinating journey that many Baby Boomers and post-Boomers have taken.

Family reunions were reintroduced to society by Baby Boomers, of whom many are amateur desktop genealogist and loving, attentive family members seeking to preserve their precious union.

The early Boomers were said to be the healthiest, more educated generation of their time, many genuinely expecting progress in world relations. The latter Boomers made use of modern technology to reach out, learn and better themselves and the world around them.

As news of world events are delivered across a more sophisticated communications network and our parents begin to expire we become ever more aware of our own mortality and the need to preserve what has been left by the preceding generations. The desire to connect and reconnect with the genealogical rootstock and its offshoots formed the rebirth of family reunion events as we've come to know them.

Family reunions fill our desire to hold on tight to the memories and wisdom entrusted to us by our loved ones. These events provide the ideal venue to remember milestones in the lives of each family member, honor surviving elders and pass on stories and legends of our ancestry to our young.

As you plan the reunion you will learn much along the way and open yourself and your family to memorable moments that will help them know they belong. The tutorial, journal and worksheets will help you plan, organize, manage and document this most memorable event. You'll also benefit from free access to Fimark's Family Reunion Planner application. See more regarding Fimark's Family Reunion Planner software on page 12.

"Somehow by grace and providence we've arrived to fall upon the bosom of all our family. To kiss warm faces and wipe the tears of joy from cheeks cracked and dimpled by time. We found our way back home."

Acknowledgements

My heartfelt appreciation and thanks go to the originator of the family, mans Creator. What wonders He has endowed upon us.

The natural instincts of a nurturing mother hosting new life. Only her breasts can provide the warmth and sustenance her young need as it is lulled by her heart beat and breathy songs that assure, secure and sedate. While fathers set protective boundaries, the child's sense of directions and guidance are balanced by mother's empathy. The two are their baby's host to a fascinating world. As it grows, freedom is granted to explore, learn and respect the wonders of the earth.

To mother, Betty-Lou, whose spirituality, love, personal interest and support are the stuff a strong house is made of. Your stories of life's lessons are gems and gold.

To my loving father, a spiritual man, hard worker and gentlemen. Graced with honor and a depth of understanding I have yet to fathom. Mother is the love of his life. They are my sense of belonging, security and identity. Thank you both for your example and love for life.

To two my sisters, whose depth of heart, loyalty and wisdom go unmatched. To my brother, whose love of the arts sparked my own creativity.

To my two sons, caring men with thinking ability. To my daughter-in-law, a fellow artist and creative spirit. A fine compliment to her husband who has given me a wonderful daughter.

To my dear wife, all warmth and light heartedness. You do not let life change you accept to add more laughter and joy to it. Thank you for adding more colors, textures and hues to the canvas of our lives.

To our beautiful and precious granddaughter, to whom we have so many of life's wonders to share.

May God continue to bless our union.

Mark Askew

Annual Family Reunion Proclamations and Observances

Family Reunion Month - A Proclamation in 1985 to raise awareness of a growing trend of runaway children and newly formed organizations to help reunite families of runaways the Congress, by House Joint Resolution 64, has designated the period May 12 to June 16, 1985, as "Family Reunion Month" and authorized and requested the President to issue a proclamation in observance of this period.

National Family Reunion Month - Commercial enterprises dubbed August as National Family Reunion Month.

National Family Reunion Month - While some commercial enterprises have dubbed August as National Family Reunion Month many social groups including churches observe National Family Reunion Month in the month of July.

Annual Family Reunion Planning Month - A family awareness group with a focus on genealogy and traditional family reunion planning established in 2005 named November as "Annual Family Reunion Planning Month". ---Mark A. Askew, Founder: Legendary Heritage Heirlooms and Fimark Home Online.

"By some miracle we all stand and look around and are reminded that ours is a union resilient and empowered by years of congealed tears of joy, love and sorrow. Braced by our own blood, comforted by our own songs we labor to find our way home... We found our way back home."

Tutorial

Planning and organizing a family reunion is perhaps one of the most engaging and fulfilling projects you will ever embark upon. Like planning a wedding there are likely to be small gatherings and meetings throughout the year in order to discuss and execute action items leading to the annual event. These small get-togethers and meetings are what really help to bring loved ones together for one common cause, and are therefore a uniting bond.

Starting the plans for a family reunion is much like trying to ride a bike for the first time. Remember how learning to stay on that bike and keep your balance was both exciting and terrifying all at the same time? But with a little perseverance your confidence grew and before you knew it you were coasting down-hill. The purpose of this family reunion planning guide is to help you plan we well balanced plan you can stay on top of, and eventually coast along while enjoying the ride.

That said, whether this is your first family reunion or your 50th, take the time to document your experiences while planning, organizing and managing the event. Your Family Reunion Planner includes "My Family Reunion Planning Journal" on page 38. Use it to record the highlights, projects and wisdom learned along the way. Record gems that you'll always want to remember, use and passed on to the next generation.

Reunion Planning Elements
Four key issues need to be considered while planning your family reunion: What is your mission? What will the theme of the event be? Who will be honored? Which homestead will be the point of focus? You will also need to consider the best location for family activities and dining.

Meals and Menu
The Family Reunion Planner provides a meals and menu forms for each day of the event as well as recipe templates for recording traditional family recipes for breakfast, lunch and dinner. Learn about fun and exciting to prepare for the family reunion that will help record your meal plan on page 85 and exchange and record recipes on page 90.

Getting the Word Out
Take advantage of email, online messengers, newsletters and word-of-mouth to let all family members know the family is having a reunion. Other ideas to let others know you're planning a family reunion event are announcement sites located at most Internet family reunion web resources. There is an announcement letter and survey form found on pages 117 and 122.

Timing Is Everything
Remember to give family members plenty of notice. 12 months advance notice will allow attendees to plan some of their vacation time around the event. Make

good use of the Advance Family Reunion Planner Timeline on page 15 to guide you thru the 12 month planning process.

Reunion Planning Committee
If you're planning a big reunion event, you do well to put together a reunion committee. Ask for other family members to help with planning activities and choosing the time and place (this should be done first). This book provides a detailed committee organizing and managing guide found on page 12 and 68.

Planning Family Reunion Activities
Activities can be as simple as an at home get-together, a reunion in the park or a luxury cruise. Reunions that include travel and touring can be exciting and enriching. Locations to visit may include the family homestead, school house and places for family entertainment.

Activities can include historic re-enactments that stimulate family morale, challenge the intellect and fuel the imagination while enabling the viewer to see touch and hear the past. Older family members may narrate stories about the relatives that include life lessons and historic events. This can be a good time to reminisce about departed family members and recount humorous stories about their personalities. You may wish to include this in your journal.

Assign each member of your newly formed reunion committee a specific task, such as T-shirts and memorabilia, genealogy presentations including memorials and historic tours/entertainment, dining events, Reunion Book, entertainment, videographer, photography, etc. You'll find a department list with associated worksheets on page 68.

Make sure those delegated certain duties know exactly what is expected of their department and who to report to with questions. The written instructions found on the worksheets should be reviewed with each department head when assigning tasks.

Planning Entertainment
The type of entertainment you feature at your family reunion event should largely depend on the theme, slogan, those in attendance and what the majority will enjoy. First make a contact list or database of invitees. Consider what they enjoy in the form of hobbies, entertainment and amusement. All families have a common thread regarding entertainment interests. Consider entertainment that all can enjoy.

Take Charge

The most important aspect of family reunion planning is your willingness to take charge of the process from start to finish. You want to by fully committed to organizing and managing the event.

Promote It

Now that you have made the commitment you will want the rest of the family to do the same. The key is in promoting the idea of having a fun, refreshing day devoted to reuniting the family. Why not start by observing the kinds of activities that everyone already enjoys doing. Next consider the skills each member has.

While promoting the reunion make an assessment of skills, talents and interests. Remember to include these when considering activities. While some are great at cooking and catering others may be good at decorating and such. Most families have an artist and crafts-person.

Many family reunion planners take time to commend family members on their skills and talents while asking them to contribute ideas for the event. Once the ideas start pouring in you now have the ideal venue to start promoting the event. It will not be difficult to get committed volunteers when everyone is involved in the planning process.

Themes & Activity Ideas
There are a number of themes and activities that can be incorporated into the family reunion event that will make it all the more enriching and meaning. Here are just a few.

Historic Skits
The skits can highlight a pivotal point in the family's history. Participants will enjoy research period customs, dialogue, costumes, etc.

Story Telling
Family members who have the gift of story-telling can bring to life tales of ancestors and their accomplishments. Life lessons can be taught and a greater interest in family history and the ties that bind can be stimulated.

Genealogy Tours
Consider taking the family on an exciting tour of important hot spots including the homestead, the towns that family settled into, the machines they worked and street they walked as well as activities they immersed themselves into.

Genealogy Presentations
Present historic documents and vintage artifacts that center on the times and locations of ancestors.

"While we still can stand let us vow to inspire and aspire to be true to this family union not made by chance but by the love of two hearts that also managed to take a stand and build a strong house. Because of them we found our way back home."

Family Reunion Planning For Individual Coordinators

1. Your first task is to review the Family Reunion Checklist and Timeline Planner. This will give you an overall idea of all that is involved in the planning organizing and management process of the event.

2. Put together your family contact list. You'll want to make use of a reunion attendee registration contact list, spreadsheet or guest list roster. These applications are provided in Fimark's Family Reunion Planner application at www.family-reunion-planner.fimark.net

3. Start gathering initial ideas for the event after looking over the "Reunion Themes" section of this book. Once you have established themes for the event, look over the "Event Planner Worksheet", "Scheduling Worksheet" and "Possible Locations" worksheet.

4. Begin announcing that plans are underway for the next family reunion and the need to consider theme, slogan, date and location options. Send out your initial announcement using the survey worksheet on page 117.

5. Once the surveys start coming in enter the selected theme and activities options data on a survey estimator such as the one found on the Attendee Registration Panel in Fimark's Family Reunion Planner application at www.family-reunion-planner.fimark.net

6. Upon narrowing down the options for the event it's time to start considering the event location and site for the luncheon/dinner program. Visit possible locations and make use of the "Possible Locations" and "Site Location" worksheets. Having chosen the site for the reunion event you can now consider the details of the itinerary.

7. If you're using one of the "Reunion Themes" provided in this book, make use of the associated Itinerary and luncheon/dinner program ideas. Otherwise edit the "Itinerary Worksheet" on page 120 and the "Lunch/Dinner Program" provided on page 119.

8. Having established all activities and programs begin looking over tasks according to departments.

Departments

Attendants/Security
Communications Department
Decorating and Catering
Food Committee, 85, 86, 90

Health and Safety Department
Setup and Cleanup
Welcome/Greeting

continued...

Finance Department
Fundraising Page 103
Genealogy Research, 106-114
News and Media
Photography

Activities Committees

Indoor Activities, 8, 9, 78
Outdoor Activities, 8, 9, 78, 80
Music and Sound, 101
Travel and Tours Committee, 19

9. Use the "Needs List" to begin listing all supply/materials and service needs for your event with the help and feedback of department heads.

10. Create a ballpark expense list using the Budget list and Cost Estimator provided in Fimark's Family Reunion Planner application or spreadsheet workbook to estimate total costs and required dues per person.

11. Complete all worksheets and contact all vendors, suppliers, caterers and entertainers to make absolutely sure your budget is accurate before sending out mailings for reunion dues. Remember to add a few extra dollars per person for unforeseen expenses including shipping and mailing of T-shirts if requested.

12. Complete the "Event Planner Worksheet" and "Scheduling Worksheet" on pages 73 and 75.

13. Send out your invitational announcements using the template found on page 122.

14. Take time to carefully review each form in this planner. You'll notice worksheets and instructions for various departments. Add additional departmental instructions as needed before printing and distributing to departments and/or those assisting.

15. It's now time to delegate assignments to volunteers. Assign one or two persons to oversee each department. Department heads have the following duties:

- Organizing and scheduling department meetings and notifying the members of those meetings
- Maintain a list of volunteers
- Presiding over meetings and review and delegate tasks and assignments
- Keep a calendar of tasks and checklist of unfinished business
- Motivate volunteers to follow through

16. Add contact information of Department Heads on page 68.

17. Each week go thru your Advanced Family Reunion Timeline found on page 15 and the Family Reunion Checklist on page 16 and follow up on tasks assigned, vendors and related services used.

FAMILY REUNION PLANNING FOR COMMITTEES

1. Look over the Family Reunion Planning Timeline to get an idea of task assignments throughout the next 12-9 months. After looking over the "Event Planner Worksheet", "Scheduling Worksheet" and "Site Location Worksheet" commence announcing to all family members that plans are underway for the next family reunion and the need to consider ideas and select committee members and volunteers.

2. Start compiling a list of family members complete with addresses, phone numbers, email and social net accounts. An ideal contact database is found in Fimark's Family Reunion Planner application.

3. Look over the "Themes" section starting on page 19 and the "Possible Locations" form. Send out your initial announcement along with the survey found on page 117 to family members asking for their opinions and suggestions for event dates, activities and possible locations.

4. Begin choosing committee members with the help of those already onboard. Establish an initial committee meeting time and place where most can attend.

5. Form your initial committee members including the chairperson and treasurer. The following committees can be formed according to activities and needs. These can consist of one or two persons or more depending on the size of the event.

6. Use your "Committees List" worksheet on page 68 to begin selecting department heads.

Departments

Attendants/Security
Communications Department
Decorating and Catering
Food Committee, 85, 86, 90
Finance Department
Fundraising Page 103
Genealogy Research, 106-114
News and Media
Photography

Health and Safety Department
Setup and Cleanup
Welcome/Greeting

Activities Committees

Indoor Activities, 8, 9, 78
Outdoor Activities, 8, 9, 78, 80
Music and Sound, 101
Travel and Tours Committee, 19

7. Now review your "Consideration Elements" along with the "Reunion Themes" section found on pages 19 - 36. As you discuss "Consideration Elements" found

on page 76, record final decisions as to who will do what and delegate department heads and volunteers accordingly. Make sure delegations are in harmony with the skills required for each department. Avoid overlapping assignments.

8. Using the returned surveys you sent out in the initial mailing start entering survey options data regarding most voted activities and desired location on a worksheet. You'll find an ideal survey options calculation worksheet, "Reunion Attendee Registration Worksheet and Guest List Roster" in Fimark's Family Reunion Planner application at www.family-reunion-planner.fimark.net. If you end up with activities and location option ties take a vote at the next committee meeting.

9. Now it's time to visit site locations to determine appropriate venues to hold the event. Complete the "Event Planner Worksheet" and "Scheduling Worksheet" to the extent that you can. Upon visiting the possible locations make us of the "Site Location Worksheet" found on pages 73 - 75.

10. Use the "Needs List" on page 82 to begin listing all supply/materials and service needs for your event with the help and feedback of department heads.

11. Complete the "Agenda Planning for Lunch/Dinner Program", as wells as the Meals and Menus Form on pages 85 and 86.

12. Create a ballpark expense list using the Budget List and Cost Estimator provided in Fimark's Family Reunion Planner application or spreadsheet workbook to estimate total costs and required dues per person.

13. Complete all worksheets and contact all vendors, suppliers, caterers and entertainers to make absolutely sure your budget is accurate before sending out mailings for reunion dues. Remember to add a few extra dollars per person for unforeseen expenses including shipping and mailing of T-shirts if requested.

14. If you're using one of the "Reunion Themes" provided in this book, make use of the associated Itinerary and luncheon/dinner program ideas. Otherwise edit the "Itinerary Worksheet" on page 120 and the "Luncheon/Dinner Program" provided on page 119.

15. Send out your invitational announcements using the template found on page 122. Find colorful invitations at www.family-reunion-planner.fimark.net

16. Take time to carefully review each form in this planner. You'll notice worksheets and instructions for various departments. Add additional departmental instructions as needed before printing and distributing to departments and/or those assisting.

17. Using your "Committee List" on page 68, "Follow-up Notes" on page 70 and "Department Worksheets" starting on page 78, contact all department heads

several weeks in advance to remind them to complete delegated tasks according to the time line.

18. Hand out the "Reunion Evaluation Form" to all coordinators, department heads and volunteers before the final committee meeting (scheduled on the final day of the reunion).

19. Compile a list of commendations and a list of suggested improvements from the evaluation forms collected. During your final committee meeting, review evaluation feedback when making plans for your next family reunion.

20. Each week go thru your Advanced Family Reunion Timeline found on page 15 and the Family Reunion Checklist on page 17 and follow up on tasks assigned, vendors and related services used.

**"Let's celebrate life
and drink up the day
making time stand still for but a moment
and then spend the rest of our days
remembering sweetly from where we have come
now that we have found our way back home."**

ADVANCED FAMILY REUNION PLANNING TIME LINE

One year in Advance:

- Commence compiling a reunion journal containing ideas, suggestions, communications, records, etc.
- Establish events and activities characteristic of family's interests
- Compile an e-mail and postal mail list
- Develop reunion committees
- Contact tourism bureaus, chambers of commerce, and convention and visitors bureaus for meeting facilities, accommodations, dining, attraction, and event information

One Year in Advance:

- Mail out requests for genealogy research help and reunion suggestions including theme, approximate cost, tentative plans, etc.
- Set a reunion events date
- Choose location and make reservations
- Choose for photographer/videographer, caterer, entertainment, etc.

Six to Nine Months in Advance:

- Send formal event invitations that include the date, time, and directions/map to location; directions/map to available accommodations; a registration form (RSVP); updated 'missing persons' list; itinerary; fundraising activities; and any other related information which will be helpful in assisting each members participation
- Confirm all reservations and appointments with photographer/videographer, caterer, entertainers, etc
- Choose your menu, or confirm dining arrangements
- Continue to send invitations to people as they are located
- Hold fund raiser to treasury holding for current and future events

Four Months in Advance:

- Choose theme, decorations, banners, etc.
- Visit and survey locations for reunion activities and accommodations with the entire reunion committee and meet with the Reunion Consultant
- Reserve necessary rental equipment

- Submit order for t-shirts or souvenirs, decorations
  http://family-reunion-t-shirts.fimark.net

Six Weeks in Advance:

- Complete the directory/memory book and have printed
- Have committee leaders get together and form a reunion day checklist
- Order Welcome Baskets for each room reserved
- Assign tasks to anyone who has volunteered to assist

Two Weeks in Advance:

- Review final checklist
- Purchase all last minute necessities such as decorations, souvenirs, supplies

The Day Before Reunion Event:

- Review progress/incidentals with committee leaders and make a note of follow-up on page 70
- Meet with facility managers and make a list of staff contacts for assistance and emergencies

Morning of Event(s):

- Arrive Early
- Decorate and set up necessary equipment and supplies
- Welcome reunion members
- Have fun, relax, and enjoy the fruits of all your hard work!

Final Committee Meeting

- Meet with committee leaders and note in your journal any information which will be helpful when planning your next reunion. Nominate a new reunion coordinator to begin planning the next big event
- Send a couple of your favorite event photos to be included on Reunion web page
- Continued on the bottom of page 69
-

"In every heart beat
they beat death and live
in our laughter, in our song,
in our very being they find their way back home."

A FAMILY REUNION PLANNING CHECKLIST

1. Appoint a coordinator for the event ☐

    a. ___ Plan and organize well beforehand
    b. ___ Rely on the needs and desires of your extended family
    c. ___ Notify the extended family that "we're all going to get together"
    d. ___ Track down the relatives, including relatives out of the country

2. Make a master list many months ahead of planned event ☐

    a. ___ Consult relatives for distant relatives' names and addresses
    b. ___ Use older family members as sources of information and family history
    c. ___ Look through family albums, old letters, etc.
    d. ___ Use a personal ad in local papers telling of the reunion

3. Create a family file for current and future use ☐

    a. ___ Names, addresses, telephone numbers, e-mail
    b. ___ Occupations (this information may be helpful, for example, you may have a cousin who's a DJ or an Aunt in the catering business)
    c. ___ Start creating family line, for example, second cousin, great uncle, etc.
    d. ___ Consider special interests such as hobbies, spare time activities, etc.

4. Help ☐

    a. ___ Involve relatives, thereby, creating a greater interest
    b. ___ Organize teams or committees for the various tasks
    c. ___ Finances – Consider Fund Raiser Drives for raising funds
    d. ___ Food and lodging
    e. ___ Activities and entertainment
    f. ___ Collecting family memorabilia
    g. ___ Creating a family tree and/or history
    h. ___ Miscellaneous details
    i. ___ Appeal to people's interests and abilities
    j. ___ Recruit a liaison for each branch of the family to:
        i. ___ Keep each branch up to date
        ii. ___ Give head count of who will attend
        iii. ___ Relay information to each of the teams

5. Keep a reunion notebook ☐

    a. ___ Add or delete pages as necessary
    b. ___ Assign a separate section to each team
    c. ___ Decrease chance of snafus, misunderstandings, and disappointments

6. Planning the event ☐

    a. One rule: The affair should suit your family's interest and needs
    b. ___ When should the event occur? In conjunction with other events in the area
    c. Allow relatives sufficient time to make arrangements
    d. ___ Emphasize special significance of gathering together as a family
    e. ___ Take a family reunion options survey:
        i. How long for the event? One day? Two days? Etc.
        ii. Special interests
        iii. Do it yourselves or let professionals do the work?
    f. ___ Site Location
    g. ___ Lodging
    h. ___ Invitations should be exciting and imaginative
    i. ___ Feeding the family
        i. ___ Caterer or family getting together to prepare the meals
        ii. ___ Be aware of any special dietary needs.

7. Enjoy yourselves ☐

    a. ___ Arrange Ice breaker activities to reacquaint and greet all relatives
    b. ___ Variety is the spice of life. Have a variety of activities for young and older
    c. ___ Strengthen memories via videotaping your reunion
    d. ___ Family history. Write it down and print it up
    e. ___ Your reunion is a good time to compile or update the family tree

8. Establish a tradition ☐

    a. ___ Keep in touch with the relatives with whom you reconnect at the reunion
    b. ___ Start a family newsletter
    c. ___ Plan the next reunion
    d. ___ Do not let it stop here!
    e. ___ Get a Family Reunion Website to upload family reunion pictures, video, special announcements

REUNION THEMES

Choose a theme and for your event and work out the basic activities, itinerary and luncheon/dinner program.

Family Reunion Culture Fest Planner – Select family members for Genealogy DNA tests. Inform all that the results will be revealed at the Family Reunion Culture Fest. Using your genealogy research results, pay homage to the varied lands, cultures, times and places that combine to make you who you are. Page 31

Family Reunion Genealogy City Tour Planner - Learn the beginnings of your roots while on tour from the Deep South to the Industrial North. Chart the course and travel to places that will answer questions you never thought to ask. Page 34

Family Reunion Living Legends Ball Planner - Throw a spectacular event to honor the elder African-American men and women of your family who have paved the way for others. Page 36

Family Reunion Luxury Cruise Planner - Cruise Ships are spectacular floating resorts filled with dozens of unique settings for swimming, dancing, dining. Page 20

"And so we lengthen the tent cords and raise the tent cloths
to bring together all their progeny.
Let the memory of our mothers and fathers laid to rest live strong in us
and thus we bring them home.
We bring them all back home."

FAMILY REUNION CRUISE

Overview

Cruise Ships are spectacular floating resorts filled with dozens of unique venues for relaxation, recreation and dining.

Unwind and relax at Spas, pools, golf greens and dinner shows or just soak in the sun and water spray. Tour exotic beaches, hold family banquet programs and get cozy in your cabin.

Activities and amenities usually included in family reunion packages:

- Welcome Letter from the Captain
- Private Banquets
- In-Room Meals
- Movies
- Shows
- Golf
- Ship Tours
- Aqua Park Passes or Rock Climbing Session
- Deluxe Photo Package
- Door or Bed Decorations
- Personalized Cake or Event Keepsakes and Favors

You'll find great family reunion cruise planning tips and ideas at www.family-reunion-planner.fimark.net.

Family Reunion Cruise Tips

The following information will help you prepare an enjoyable family reunion on a luxury cruise line. This planner features cruise ships amenities, reunion cruise activities and suggestions ideal for small or large groups of 15 – 300 or more.

1. Gather cruise brochures from a travel agency, or check out cruise offers, ships and deck plans online. These will give you a good idea of destinations, prices, types of accommodations, amenities and recreational options.

2. Figure out where you would like to go. Talk to an expert travel agent, or simply ask get recommendations from experienced cruise vacationers. (Some popular destinations are the Caribbean, Mexico and Alaska.)

A Top Cruise Agency provides a number of benefits:

- Savings – A Cruise Specialist has strong relationships with all cruise lines and uses the latest in computer reservations systems to enable our agents and our websites to access the most up-to-date cruise deals.
- Information – Cruise resources provide accurate information relevant to your cruise vacation with price discounts packages and cheap services.
- Expertise – Your Cruise Expert should work with you, both online and off, to find the best cruise and best rate that fits your interests. The person should have years of personal travel experience.
- Network of Choices – Your agency should represent all major cruise lines on more than 150 ships to over 10,000 itineraries around the world.
- Online website – A good online travel resource is open 24 hours a day and is full of information that will help with your reservation and make it easy for you to contact them by telephone or email to address any questions you may have about your vacation.
- Service – Find an agency whose representatives are knowledgeable, friendly and enthusiastic about the cruise industry.

3. Decide how long you want the cruise to be. The most popular cruises last from 3 to 14 days, but lengthier cruises are available.

4. Determine how much you want to spend. Cruises come in the basic categories of budget, moderate, deluxe and ultra-deluxe. It is suggested that you compare these categories to hotels and choose which would make you most comfortable and be within your budget.

5. Contact a local travel agent or book online at http://family-reunion-planner.fimark.net/reunion-travel-vacation.html Compare packages to your budget and the type of cruise you would like to take. Tell the agent the following information:

- Past Passenger of the Cruise Line

    If you are a past guest of a particular cruise line, you may qualify for special discounts, coupons or free upgrades that are not available online. If possible, you should have your past passenger number handy when you call.

- Member of a frequent flyer club

- An AARP Member or Over the Age of 55

    Many cruise lines offers discounted rates to passengers that are traveling with at least one passenger who is an AARP Member or 55 years of age and older. The rates aren't always shown online so you must ask for it on the phone.

- Traveling with 2 or more cabins

    If you have two or more cabins traveling together, you may be able to negotiate a lower multi-cabin rate. By speaking to a live, breathing agent, not only will they work with you to find cabins near one another, but you'll get to sit together at dinner and possibly get a lower rate.

- Resident Rates

    Cruise lines will often give special discounts to residents of certain states. If a cruise line needs help filling a ship with passengers from your area, they may offer you a lower rate. Call to see if your state qualifies.

- Military – Active or Retired

    The cruise lines are very appreciative of the commitment made by our armed forces. Some extend a special military discount to members of every branch of service including immediate family members. Your military id is required.

- Other Discounts

    If you are an Educator, in Public Service, a member of a Wholesale Shopping Club, an American Express Platinum Card holder, a MasterCard holder or a member of a Credit Union, you may qualify for additional discounts.

6. Choose your point of departure, with the agent's assistance. Many cruises require that you book your own transportation to departure points, so you will need to figure this transportation as an additional cost.

7. Decide on the number of port calls - stops into port - you would prefer. This information should be available in the brochure or from the travel agent. If you plan to do organized activities at these ports, you may be charged extra.

8. Select the type of stateroom you want. Like hotel rooms, they vary in size and available services. Check the deck plan and brochure for photos of various staterooms and maps of where the staterooms are situated.

9. Ask about any cancellation fees or other restrictions.

10. Ask the travel agent to book your cruise, or book your cruise online at www.family-reunion-planner.fimark.net/reunion-travel-vacation.html.

You can get great discount fares and will have access to ship reviews and other information that will help in making all the important decisions.
Before boarding the Cruise ship you will be required complete pre-cruise registration forms with your cruise line. You will receive information about this process from your Cruise Line Customer Support Team after your final payment.

Many Cruise Line websites allow you to pre-purchase shore excursions or land tours. This is a convenient way to pre-plan your vacation activities without waiting in line at the Shore Tours Desk onboard. Ask for a list of competitively priced shore tours to the Caribbean, Alaska, and the Bahamas on our site.

When checking in at your cruise ship you will be required to provide proper proof of US Citizenship. You should be prepared to present a certified copy of your birth certificate with a photo id. For international travel, you will be required to have a passport. For complete details, visit the Immigration Requirements section of the website. Your Cruise expert should take time to review specific ID requirements at the time of booking.

Family Reunion Cruise Planner

Number Attending:	
Cruise Line:	
Destination:	
Rendezvous location:	
Rendezvous Time	
Boarding Time:	
Number of Days:	From: To:
Package Type:	
Theme:	
Slogan:	
Activities:	

Day 1: Activities	Morning	Noon	Evening	Other

Day 2: Activities	Morning	Noon	Evening	Other

Day 3: Activities	Morning	Noon	Evening	Other

Day 4:	Morning	Noon	Evening	Other
Activities				

Day 5:	Morning	Noon	Evening	Other
Activities				

Day 6:	Morning	Noon	Evening	Other
Activities				

Day 7:	Morning	Noon	Evening	Other
Activities				

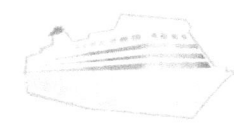

Cruise Travelers Checklist

	Swimsuit
	Swimsuit "cover-up"
	Shorts
	Reunion t-shirts
	Sun hat/reunion cap
	Sandals
	Casual wear
	camera accessories
	Flash cards
	Formal wear
	Camera/video recorder
	Dressy casual wear
	Formal evening wear
	Film
	binoculars
	Batteries
	Sun lotion
	After sun lotion
	Insect repellent
	Small bottles of: shower gel, shampoo, conditioner
	Small empty bottles/jars to decant cosmetics.
	band aids
	Sun hat
	Ear plugs
	Paperback books
	Mp3/mobile phone
	Water wallet/wet and dry case
	Small bottle laundry detergent
	Boiled sweets/mints
	"safe wallet"/money belt
	First aid kit
	Makeup kit
	mints
	toiletries
	Socks/shoes

Cruise Timeline Planner

Six months before you cruise:

Ensure that your passport does not expire six months after your time of travel. Some countries require a period of up to six months before expiry on your passport.

Find out if the cruise line will process any needed visas. Find out lead times and make necessary arrangements.

If you have booked a "cruise-only" fare you will need to make your own flight arrangements. You'll want to fly to your departure port the day before you sail. If you are a member of a frequent flyer club, provide this information when booking.

Make your hotel arrangements if you have booked a "cruise-only" fare. If you are in a hotel's frequent-guest program, provide this information when booking.

Are you a member of your cruise line's past passenger program? Ensure that your travel agent and/or the cruise line have your membership number and that you enter it on your pre-cruise registration forms.

Three months before you cruise:

Look into your cruise line's shore excursion program as published on the internet. If you're looking for a good place to start go to…
www.family-reunion-planner.fimark.net/reunion-travel-vacation.html.

Travel publications may feature information on independent tours. Book the ship's sponsored excursion immediately as bookings may become filled before you board.

Some travel areas require vaccinations. Visit your clinic months in advance as some vaccination become "effective" months after treatment.

Apply for travel insurance if not included in your cruise package. Consider taking out an annual travel insurance policy if you plan to travel more than one time this year.

Two months before you cruise:

Make final payments on your cruise. Expect to receive your cruise tickets three weeks before your cruise.

If you are driving yourself to the port or airport, contact port/airport parking facilities and book parking.

Purchase bus/coach transfer or train ticket to your departure port or airport.

One month before you cruise:

Retrieve your cruise tickets in the mail. Inspect dates and other details for accuracy including assigned the cabin, dinner seating, luggage labels

Make certain the cruise line has made any air or hotel arrangements for you, that these are correct and that the flight tickets and hotel vouchers are enclosed.

Look for an assortment of cruise lines and discount group rates at www.family-reunion-planner.fimark.net/reunion-travel-vacation.html

Make your home/pet/children/parent-sitting/newspaper-picking up and houseplant watering arrangements. Arrange to have newspaper and other deliveries stopped if appropriate.

Provide emergency contact information including the ship's telephone, fax number.

Get your car serviced is you will be driving it to port.

Complete any pre-boarding Passenger Information forms that the cruise line requires. Online applications submit immediately to the database where "hard-copy" may sit for weeks, even months before processing.

Two weeks before you cruise:

Pick out your cruise clothes

Pickup dry cleaning

Pack all items

Now is the time to make sure everything fits in your suitcase

Polish/clean shoes

Gather vitamins, over-the-counter and prescription medicines that you require.

Purchase and pack up eyeglasses/sunglasses or contact lenses and solution

One week before you cruise:

Get your hair done.

Do your laundry.

Get your foreign currency/travelers checks. Remember to have enough funds for tipping.

If flying, re-check your flight times and check-in times via the phone or Internet.

Phone your credit card company and tell them where you'll be traveling.

Copy your credit card and write down the issuers' emergency phone numbers.

Leave a copy of this along with photocopy of your passport at home with someone you trust.

Three days before you cruise:

Do your ironing.

Complete luggage labels with your name and cabin number.

Two days before you cruise:

Book your taxi to the airport/pier/train station.

Provide empty clothes bags for soiled clothes.

Pack a flashlight, particularly if you will be in an inside cabin (no windows, no natural light).

Place a sheet of paper with your name, flight and cruise details and travel dates and your home/mobile telephone number and address into your suitcase before you close it. This is in case your luggage labels or other external identifiers are torn off.

The night before you leave:

Prepare your handbag/overnight bag:

Checklist

Passport

Photocopy of your passport

- Cruise tickets
- Air tickets
- Hotel confirmation voucher
- Car rental confirmation voucher
- Driving license
- Travel insurance documents including the policy number and emergency assistance phone number
- Currency/travelers checks
- Credit cards
- Note of credit card emergency numbers
- Diary/address book with addresses for postcards and emergency contact numbers
- Membership cards
- Eyeglasses/reading glasses/sunglasses
- Prescription medications
- Valuables/jewelry
- Camera
- Ear plugs
- Handkerchief/tissues
- Synchronize all clock and set alarms

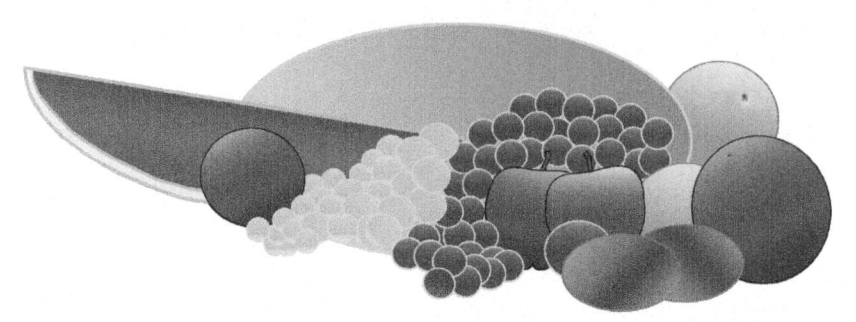

Family Fest Planner
A Family Reunion Cultural Festival

Overview

Throw a Festival rich in culture, colorful garb and tradition. Using your genealogy research results take a virtual tour of the varied lands, cultures, times and places that combine to make your family what it is today. Celebrate the center where connecting lines meet at the Family Reunion Fest of Colors.

A rich heritage from around the world combines African culture with that of Native American Indians and European migration. Your cultural expo begins with genealogy research. Fimark's Genealogy Research Tool Kit helps you discover hidden treasures about your past easily and quickly using tools and research methods of expert historians. Go the extra one thousand miles using modern DNA testing and get a perfect lineage match in a matter of weeks.

Research your family lineage up to the 21th century. Consider using DNA technology to fill in the gaps 300 – 400 years or more. Note intersecting cultures, collect artifacts, exotic recipes, costumes and stories that tell the tale.

Select family members to exhibit costumes, tell stories and tour the artifacts. Have historic reenactments, teach and enjoy cultural dance sessions and learn to cook exotic cuisine.

Presentations and Program

1. Genealogy Research Presentations and Entertainment

    DNA Genealogy Results Presentations (Several weeks in advance get

    DNA tests of elders or their progeny and present the results at the reunion event)

    Cultural Music CD or Live Band

Cultural Dance Video or Dance Group

Presentation of Colorful Cultural Garb

Artifacts Table Presenting tools, toys, jewelry

Reenactment group to recount historic events that impacted the families' migration from place to place.

3. **Table of Cultural Recipes**

    Contributed recipes from distant lands, cities and times.
    3 or more cooking tables to demonstrate how to whip up international sweet treats, exotic cuisine and how to put it all together using unique cooking utensils

4. **Our Legendary Heritage in Pictures**

    Display 20 jumbo sized photographs of family members from around the world. Feature excerpts of pages telling your family history from the present to the past and all the adventure, love, romance, drama, war and intrigue along the way.

    Story Telling: The Storyteller uses the images to paint a poignant and inspiring tale in pictures and stories about family legends past and present.

5. **Awards to Elders**

    Present certificates of achievement to elders of the family

6. **Poem Recitals**

    This segment of the event can include poetry written by artists in the family or recitals from such poets as Dr. Maya Angelou or Mark Askew.

7. **Entertainment**

    Provide a Band, talent show or feature last years family reunion video projected on big screen.

Family Reunion Culture Fest continued.

8. Singing

Local talent or invited celebrity

9. Family Dance

The traditional family dance

10. Closing Comments from MC and Chairperson

The MC thanks all for coming and thanks those who helped put things together. Music plays while guests mingle and chat.

Notes:

_____
_____
_____
_____
_____
_____
_____
_____
_____
_____

Genealogy Homestead Tour Planner

Overview

Learn the beginnings of your roots while on tour. Travel from the motherland and follow the migration of your family from past to present. Make use of DNA genealogy technology to chart the course and travel to places that will answer questions you never thought to ask.

Using your DNA and genealogy research results pay homage to the motherland, the varied cities, cultures, times and places that combine to make you who you are today.

Activities

Announcement that DNA results will be announced at Ballroom Dinner. Visit cities and towns where a treasure of knowledge reveals the secrets of the inner self: *Who we are; Why we are;* and *Where we've come*. Visit museums and collect artifacts, recipes, costumes and stories that tell the tale.

Reunion Tour Itinerary

1. Meet and Greet in Hotel Lobby
Make sure all have the Dinner Program

2. Early Evening Dining in Ball Room
   -- Welcome from Committee Chairperson
   -- Welcome from The Mayor or Hotel Manager/Award to Mayor
   -- A motivational speech can be given highlighting life's journey from one generation to the next. DNA research announced.

3. Award the Eldest Family Members

4. The Itinerary is read. T-shirts and tour program distributed.

5. The Tour
10 a.m. Tour Buses pick up family members next morning and commence sight-seeing stops on the way to Brunch. After Brunch tour continues toward shopping district.

6. Shopping and Sight-Seeing
1 p.m. break for snacks relaxation and shopping.

7. Hotel Drop Off
4 p.m. tourist pickup and drop off at hotel.

8. Pool Party
5:30 p.m. Kids enjoy pizza pool party and get acquainted

9. Next Day
Breakfast at 9 a.m.

11 a.m. Tour Buses pick up family

Tour commences at cultural museum highlighting the work, music and activities of ancestors, land marks significant to heritage
Cemetery lots to read stone heads of ancestors and reminisce
Tour ends at 4 p.m.

7 p.m. Dining Event with Entertainment

- Awards to elders
- Poem recitals
- Singing
- Family dance

10. Closing comments from MC and Chairperson

The MC thanks all for coming and those who helped put things together. Music plays while guest mingle and chat.

Notes:

The Smiths are having a Ball!
A Living Legends Ball!

" I cried from the beginning to the very end..."

"I was so overwhelmed to learn how my family elders helped paved the way for us."

Overview

The Living Legends Ball is a dignified inspiring white/black tie and evening gown Gala event

1. Limo Pickup

Have a limousine pickup each Legend to the ballroom. Put together a CD of all the most popular songs from musical Broadway shows and favorite artists of the past to play in the car as they ride to the Ballroom.

2. The Hostess Welcome

As the honored guests arrive by Limo they are greeted by the Officiate/Hostess and led in to the lobby for a brief welcome.

Honorees served cocktails and beverages by waiters and young'uns.

3. Honorees Escorted into Ballroom

Honored guests are lined up according to Legends-list and announced when escorted into Ballroom and seated by young'uns.

4. Master of Ceremonies Welcome
A welcome to Honored guests, husbands, young'uns and friends.
Live jazz band serenades as guests wine and dine.

5. Poetry Recital

This "thank you" segment of the event can include poetry written by artists in the family or entertain recitals from poets such as Mark Askew, Dr. Maya Angelou or others. Celebrate the spirit of family, divine guidance, brother and sisterhood, men and women of courage, and resilience.

6. The Hostess is invited by the MC to read the words engraved on a plaque highlighting loving acts of Living Legends that helped preserve their heritage. They may also choose to recite the poem "Legends Live Among Us". The plaque is awarded to the eldest Living Legend. While applauding, dessert is served with a special gift for each living legend. The Legends are asked not to open the gifts until all have been served. Once all are served, Living Legends are free to open the gifts. (Gifts may include jewelry custom engraved in honor of the event. The letters LL 2020 or words such as "Living Legend 2014 can be engraved on a heart locket, bracelet, watch, billfold, pocket knife, pen set, etc.)

7. Honored Guests Interviewed

During the Ball take some of the honored guests aside for a 2 minute video interview of how they are enjoying the event and what it means to them.

8. Living Legends Honorees Dance

Honorees are invited to the dance floor to demonstrate the dances of Living Legends while other talented Living legends take to the microphone to serenade the audience.

9. Living Legends Spouses or Close Friends are Invited to the Dance Floor

10. Young'uns are Invited to the Dance Floor

11. Honor with Lights, A Kiss and Gratitude
Honorees are asked to be seated. After all Honorees have been seated lights are dimmed. A talented Young'un is given the microphone and sings the first stanza of a song that says, "We Thank You" while Young'uns form a closed circle on the dance floor and are secretively each given a lit rose. As the song continues each Young'un now breaks the circle and gives the rose to an elder and tenderly kisses an elder on the cheek whispering "thank you".

The MC and Hostess thank the Living Legends, Their loving companions in life, family and friends, all are thanked for coming as well as those who helped put things together. Music plays while guests mingle and chat and are escorted to their cars. The teens should help the elders with their coats.

My Family Reunion Journal

Reunion Event Date: _____
Journal Start Date: _____

Journal

Date: _____

Highlights:
_____
_____
_____

Details:
_____
_____
_____
_____
_____
_____
_____
_____
_____
_____
_____
_____
_____

Journal

Date: _____

Highlights:
_____
_____
_____

Details:
_____
_____
_____
_____
_____
_____
_____
_____
_____
_____
_____
_____
_____
_____

Journal

Date: _____

Highlights:
_____
_____
_____

Details:
_____
_____
_____
_____
_____
_____
_____
_____
_____
_____
_____
_____
_____
_____
_____

Journal

Date: _____

Highlights:
_____
_____
_____

Details:
_____
_____
_____
_____
_____
_____
_____
_____
_____
_____
_____
_____
_____
_____

Journal

Date: _____

Highlights:
_____
_____
_____

Details:
_____
_____
_____
_____
_____
_____
_____
_____
_____
_____
_____
_____
_____
_____

Journal

Date: _____

Highlights:
_____
_____
_____

Details:
_____
_____
_____
_____
_____
_____
_____
_____
_____
_____
_____
_____
_____
_____

Journal

Date: _____

Highlights:
_____
_____
_____

Details:
_____
_____
_____
_____
_____
_____
_____
_____
_____
_____
_____
_____
_____
_____

Journal

Date: _____

Highlights:

_____

_____

_____

Details:

_____

_____

_____

_____

_____

_____

_____

_____

_____

_____

_____

_____

_____

_____

Journal

Date: _____

Highlights:
_____
_____
_____

Details:
_____
_____
_____
_____
_____
_____
_____
_____
_____
_____
_____
_____
_____

Journal

Date: _____

Highlights:
_____
_____
_____

Details:
_____
_____
_____
_____
_____
_____
_____
_____
_____
_____
_____
_____
_____
_____
_____

Journal

Date: _____

Highlights:
_____
_____
_____
_____

Details:
_____
_____
_____
_____
_____
_____
_____
_____
_____
_____
_____
_____
_____

Journal

Date: _____

Highlights:
_____
_____
_____

Details:
_____
_____
_____
_____
_____
_____
_____
_____
_____
_____
_____
_____
_____
_____
_____
_____

Journal

Date: _____

Highlights:
_____
_____
_____

Details:
_____
_____
_____
_____
_____
_____
_____
_____
_____
_____
_____
_____
_____
_____

Journal

Date: _____

Highlights:
_____
_____
_____

Details:
_____
_____
_____
_____
_____
_____
_____
_____
_____
_____
_____
_____
_____

Journal

Date: _____

Highlights:
_____
_____
_____

Details:
_____
_____
_____
_____
_____
_____
_____
_____
_____
_____
_____
_____
_____

Journal

Date: _____

Highlights:
_____
_____
_____

Details:
_____
_____
_____
_____
_____
_____
_____
_____
_____
_____
_____
_____
_____

Journal

Date: _____

Highlights:

_____
_____
_____

Details:

_____
_____
_____
_____
_____
_____
_____
_____
_____
_____
_____
_____
_____
_____

Journal

Date: _____

Highlights:

_____
_____
_____

Details:

_____
_____
_____
_____
_____
_____
_____
_____
_____
_____
_____
_____
_____

Journal

Date: _____

Highlights:

_____

_____

_____

Details:

_____

_____

_____

_____

_____

_____

_____

_____

_____

_____

_____

_____

_____

Journal

Date: _____

Highlights:

_____
_____
_____

Details:

_____
_____
_____
_____
_____
_____
_____
_____
_____
_____
_____
_____
_____
_____

Journal

Date: _____

Highlights:
_____
_____
_____

Details:
_____
_____
_____
_____
_____
_____
_____
_____
_____
_____
_____
_____
_____
_____

Journal

Date: _____

Highlights:

_____
_____
_____

Details:

_____
_____
_____
_____
_____
_____
_____
_____
_____
_____
_____
_____
_____
_____

Journal

Date: _____

Highlights:

_____
_____
_____

Details:

_____
_____
_____
_____
_____
_____
_____
_____
_____
_____
_____
_____
_____
_____

Journal

Date: _____

Highlights:
_____
_____
_____

Details:
_____
_____
_____
_____
_____
_____
_____
_____
_____
_____
_____
_____
_____

Journal

Date: _____

Highlights:
_____
_____
_____

Details:
_____
_____
_____
_____
_____
_____
_____
_____
_____
_____
_____
_____
_____

Journal

Date: _____

Highlights:
_____
_____
_____

Details:
_____
_____
_____
_____
_____
_____
_____
_____
_____
_____
_____
_____
_____
_____

Journal

Date: _____

Highlights:
_____
_____
_____

Details:
_____
_____
_____
_____
_____
_____
_____
_____
_____
_____
_____
_____
_____
_____

Journal

Date: _____

Highlights:
_____
_____
_____

Details:
_____
_____
_____
_____
_____
_____
_____
_____
_____
_____
_____
_____

Journal

Date: _____

Highlights:
_____
_____
_____

Details:
_____
_____
_____
_____
_____
_____
_____
_____
_____
_____
_____
_____
_____

REUNION COMMITTEES LIST

COMMITTEE/DEPARTMENT HEADS

DEPARTMENT	NAMES	PHONE(S)	EMAIL
Finance/Fundraising:	_____	_____	_____
Food Committee:	_____	_____	_____
Invitation/Communication:	_____	_____	_____
Family History:	_____	_____	_____
Entertainment/Activities:	_____	_____	_____
Set-up Committee:	_____	_____	_____
Clean-up Committee:	_____	_____	_____
Registration/ Welcoming Committee:	_____	_____	_____
Decorating Committee:	_____	_____	_____
Photography/ Recording:	_____	_____	_____

Other Committees/Departments

_____:	_____	_____	_____
_____:	_____	_____	_____
_____:	_____	_____	_____
_____:	_____	_____	_____
_____:	_____	_____	_____
_____:	_____	_____	_____
_____:	_____	_____	_____

DEPARTMENTAL ASSIGNMENT WORKSHEETS

Hand Out the Following Worksheets (starting on page 78) to the Appropriate Departments

Worksheet	Department
Hotel Booking Cost Comparison Sheet	Travel and Tours Committee
Hotel Accommodations	Travel and Tours Committee
Activities Tips Sheet	Activities Committee
Maps/Directions Sheet	Chairperson
Invitations/Flyer	Greeting Committee
Luncheon/Dinner Program	Chairperson and Activities Committee Food Committee
Meals/Menu	Food Committee
Music Selection Sheet	Music and Sound Committee
Reunion Evaluation	Chairperson
Next Reunion event Planner	Chairperson
Agenda For Luncheon/Dinner Program	
Activities Worksheet	Activities Committee
Awards/Certificates	Activities Committee
Genealogy Research and Presentation Documents	Genealogy Research and Presentation Committee

1. Using your "Committee List" on page 68, "Follow-up Notes" on page 70 and "Department Worksheets" starting on page 78, contact all department heads several weeks in advance to remind them to complete delegated tasks according to the time line.

2. Hand out the "Reunion Evaluation Form" to all coordinators, department heads and volunteers before the final committee meeting (scheduled on the final day of the reunion).

3. Compile a list of commendations and a list of suggested improvements from the evaluation forms collected. During your final committee meeting, review evaluation feedback when making plans for you next family reunion.

FOLLOW UP NOTES

FOLLOW UP DATE:

Department:_____

_____

_____

FOLLOW UP DATE:

Department:_____

_____

_____

FOLLOW UP DATE:

Department:_____

_____

_____

FOLLOW UP DATE:

Department:_____

_____

_____

FOLLOW UP DATE:

Department:_____

_____

_____

FOLLOW UP DATE:

Department:_____

_____

_____

FOLLOW UP DATE:

Department: _____

_____

_____

FOLLOW UP DATE:

Department: _____

_____

_____

FOLLOW UP DATE:

Department: _____

_____

_____

FOLLOW UP DATE:

Department: _____

_____

_____

FOLLOW UP DATE:

Department: _____

_____

_____

FOLLOW UP DATE:

Department: _____

_____

_____

FOLLOW UP DATE:

Department: _____

_____

_____

FOLLOW UP DATE:

Department: _____

_____

_____

FOLLOW UP DATE:

Department: _____

_____

_____

FOLLOW UP DATE:

Department: _____

_____

_____

FOLLOW UP DATE:

Department: _____

_____

_____

FOLLOW UP DATE:

Department: _____

_____

_____

EVENT PLANNER WORK SHEET

Date of Event:	Day of Week:	Time:	
Location Site:		Estimated # of People:	
Address of Site:		Estimated # of Invitations:	
Contact Person #1:			
Home Phone:	Mobile:	E-mail:	
Contact Person #2:			
Home Phone:	Mobile:	E-mail:	
Theme Colors:	Family Reunion Website:		
	Theme: Slogan: Details:		

SITE LOCATION WORKSHEET

Location: (For family Reunion Cruises Go To Next Page)			
Address:			
Contact Person:			Phone:
Web Site Address:			Fax:
Time Frame:			
Base Rental Fee:	Fee Per Extra Hour:		Extra Time:
Pre-set up allowed: Yes ☐ No ☐	Set-up Time:		Fee:
Clean-up Fee:	Security Fee:		Fee for Tables:
Fee for Chairs:	Number of Tables Needed:		Number of Chairs Needed:
Fee for Table Clothes:	TV/Monitors Yes ☐ No ☐		Sound System Yes ☐ No ☐
Alcoholic Beverages Allowed? Yes ☐ No ☐	Electrical Outlets Needed: How many? _____ Number of Restrooms ____		On-site Caterer: Yes ☐ No ☐ Allow Us To Bring Food? Yes ☐ No ☐
Other Services/ Amenities:	Yes No		Yes No	Notes/Other Requirements:
Handicap Accessible	☐ ☐	Outdoor Pool	☐ ☐	
Handicap Parking	☐ ☐	Lake	☐ ☐	
Plenty of Parking	☐ ☐	Fishing	☐ ☐	
RV Parking	☐ ☐	Tennis Courts	☐ ☐	
Kitchen	☐ ☐	Basketball Courts	☐ ☐	
Play area	☐ ☐	Golf	☐ ☐	
Covered outdoor area	☐ ☐	Pool Table	☐ ☐	
Pavilion	☐ ☐	Horseback Riding	☐	
Piano		Nearby Park	☐ ☐	
Meeting Rooms		Volleyball	☐ ☐	
		Miniature Golf	☐ ☐	
		Shopping Mall	☐ ☐	

SCHEDULING WORKSHEET

RSVP Due Date:	Final Head Count:	Delivery Dates/Times:
Setup Time/Date:	Clean-up Time:	Rental Pickup Date/Time: Tables: _____ Chairs: _____ Table Clothes: _____
Other:	Other:	Other:

CONSIDERATION ELEMENTS

Consideration/Element	Comments/Decisions
☐ Potential site location visited	
☐ Theme chosen	
☐ Chairperson selected for each committee	
☐ Gather cost estimates for Budget	
☐ Check for proposed date to avoid conflicts	
☐ Finalize date	
☐ Begin designing invitation	
☐ Develop press release listing for family reunion web sites	
☐ Select program entertainer, MC, family speaker	
☐ Compile mailing list, data base, e-mail listings, etc.	
☐ Investigate the need for special permits, licenses, insurance, etc.	
☐ Select photographer/videographer for event; arrange for photo session and assignment	
☐ Gather written contracts for site, catering, entertainment, decorations, etc. if needed	
☐ Order plaques, certificates, trophies, other awards or gifts	
☐ Send reunion announcement in local newspapers	
☐ Determine menu with caterer and family sponsor	
☐ Mail invitations, registration forms, and other information	
☐ Put together registration/welcoming packets	
☐ Provide caterer with an estimate number of guests expected	
☐ Provide caterer with final count	
☐ Review script	
☐ Confirm transportation needs for elderly	
☐ Organize guest homes, hotel accommodations, etc.	
☐ Prepare name tags	
☐ Assign head table seating if desired	
☐ Formalize lunch program (or other program) agenda	
☐ Print program or other special handouts	
☐ Meet with committee and helpers	

☐	Write checks for payments due	
☐	Gather receipt book, mobile credit card terminal/equipment, etc.	
☐	Load up all required materials, equipment, packets, etc.	
☐	Provide or arrange transportation for VIP's and guests	
☐	Initiate a cock-tail hour for VIP's and guests	
☐	Recheck all necessary equipment	
☐	Obtain permission to set-up in advance	

ACTIVITIES WORKSHEET

Plan a central location to welcome your out-of-town guests. The first event should be a Welcome Reception. This event should be held the first night of the Reunion or the first evening of most of your family's arrival. Make sure your activities are inclusive of all family members. Be mindful of age and physical limitations when planning events.

Suggested Activities:

☐ **Amusement Park**	
☐ **Beach**	
☐ **Bowling**	
☐ **Cookout with games and music**	
☐ **Family Reunion Cruises**	
☐ **Dinner Theater**	
☐ **Go-Kart Parks**	
☐ **Hiking/Biking**	
☐ **Horseshoes**	
☐ **Miniature Golf**	
☐ **Movies**	
☐ **Museums**	
☐ **Roller Skating Party**	
☐ **Shopping Outlets or Malls**	
☐ **Tour of the City**	
☐	
☐	
☐	
☐	
☐	

Set aside at least a portion of one day for your family to just "hang out" and do whatever they want to do. The last planned activity should be a group event, i.e. dinner at a Family Style or All-You-Can-Eat Buffet Restaurant.

POSSIBLE LOCATIONS

Compare locations to desired activities

Locations: Cruise Lines Family Homestead/Estate Old Fort Historical Building Restaurant Picnic in the Park Large Home with yard space Campgrounds/RV Park Bed and Breakfast Dude Ranch Theme or Amusement Park Family Resort Area Local Hotel Union Banquet Hall Community Recreation Center	Silent Auction Raffle Family cemetery clean-up Church Service Talent Show (see Reunion Games) Family History Skit Tour opportunities Fire Works Show Time Capsule Quilting Circle Pie/Watermelon Eating Contest Outdoor Games: Horseshoes, softball, volleyball, tennis, Golf Tournament, etc. Dance Contest Guess Who? Everyone bring baby photos Old fashion sack race, egg race, balloon toss, etc. Plant a tree/bush
Activities (also see Reunion Games, next page)	
<u>Children's Activities</u> Crafts Table Color family crest/design one Board Games/Playing Cards Outdoor Games Frisbee Puppet Show Skits	<u>Remembrances</u> Family Photo Collage Family Video Home Movies Slide Show Power Point Show "This Is Your Life" Game
<u>Memory Table</u> Old memorabilia with identifiers Old Quilts Photos Documents, Marriage Certificates, etc. Old Kitchen items Newspaper clippings Old greeting cards, post cards & letters	<u>Family Reunion Conference</u> Have scheduled events during the afternoon for family members to attend such as: Genealogy Research Class Family History Information Gathering Time Interview/videotaping the elders
<u>Family Directory</u> Names, addresses, email, phone Services offered <u>Special talents</u>	<u>Name Tags</u> List name Son/daughter of Grandson/granddaughter of City, State
<u>Sign-in Registration Table</u> Guest Book Large Plastic Table Cloth with marker Ink pens Print of Large Family Tree	<u>Silent Auction/Live Auction</u> Attendees bring crafts, products and other items to raise money to benefit the next reunion or to cover the extra costs of the current reunion.

FAMILY REUNION GAMES

Many teens and adults enjoy games based on popular television shows like the Amazing Race with a twist. Here are some exciting games that are sure to be the highlight of the event.

Wet Hose Tug of War.

You'll need a hose, large pieces of tarp, a mid-size inflatable wading pool and lots of water. Choose two teams of 5. Set up this game by placing the tarp on the ground of the game area. Place the inflatable pool in the middle of the tarp with enough room for a line of five standing on the tarp on each side of the pool. Pour water on the tarp making it slippery. Pour water on the hose as well. Fill up the wading pool with water. Both teams are to grab hold of the hose. Each team's objective is to pull the entire hose from the grip of the other team members by pulling as many of them into the wading pool.

Race Track Relay (will need a race track.)

Family Reunion Olympics" with games and sports events for different age groups as well as mixed age teams. Each team selects its name/country/symbol, with banner. Immediate family members cheers on teammates during their events. It's a lot of fun.

Family Reunion Jigsaw Puzzle Race
Assemble the jig-saw puzzle. Using previous years family reunion photo create two card table sized jigsaw puzzles from the photo. Select several family members for each team to arrange the puzzles on their table. The puzzle could have a well known fact, slogan or metaphor unique to the family printed on it. The first team to arrange the puzzle enough to guess the phrase wins.

Family Reunion Spelling Bee
Spell out full names (including first, middle and surnames) of family members on family tree.

"Survivor" Style Games.
These games are meant to be played with bare feet or in sandals. The games and contestants are played within a circle or island.

Amazing Race
This very exciting game is based on televisions amazing race and is loads of fun. The race is a family vs. family competition that tests the limits of patience, self-control, unity and all that other stuff.

It's suggested that an MC cover the race live on the web using wireless web cam connected to a live internet page and viewed on a big screen TV. This one hour event takes off as family teams complete a 2-3 mile race by car, on foot and by bike with several stops, challenges and destination clues along the way.

"My Family's Got Talent" Talent Show
The talent show can feature singing, dance and other talents including stand up comedy. The audience does the judging by applause or vote.

_____
_____
_____
_____
_____
_____
_____
_____

NEEDS LIST

		Equipment/Materials/Services	Cost
	1.	Registration guest book	
	2.	DJ	
	3.	Tent rental	
	4.	Tables and Chairs	
	5.	Balloons	
	6.	Caterer	
	7.	Guest List	
	8.	Survey forms for evaluation purposes	
	9.	Name Tags and Markers	
	10.	Souvenir T-shirts, caps, jackets	
	11.	Web site	
	12.	Maps	
	13.	Welcome packet, newsletter, etc.	
	14.	Decorations	
	15.	Paper Goods	
	16.	Board Games and Playing Cards	
	17.	Sporting equipment for outdoor games	
	18.	Story teller	
	19.	Band	
	20.	Party favors	
	21.	Banner	
	22.	Flyers, invitations, letters	
	23.	Flatware, dishes, cups	
	24.	Napkins, towels, tablecloths	
	25.		
	26.		
	27.		
	28.		
	29.		
	30.		
	31.		
	32.		
	33.		
	34.		
	35.		
	36.		

Hotel Accommodations Checklist

____ Start organizing rooming accommodations for out-of-town family members at least one year in advance.

____ Determine the number and type of rooms that your guests will need.

> Do you need a dedicated area in the hotel or hospitality suite to welcome your guests? ____ Is this provided in a package rate or at separate cost? ____
>
> Do you need a banquet room for an evening event or reception? ____ What is the cost? ____
>
> Does the hotel allow food/ drink to be brought in for your welcome reception? ____ Does the hotel provide catering? ____

____ Make cost comparisons of at least five local hotels for group rates.

____ Meet with the Hotel's Group Sales Consultants to discuss your family reunion needs. Arrange to tour the facilities. Genuine hospitality should be demonstrated and courtesy should not be based on the number of expected guests. Remember, you want your family to feel welcomed.

____ Ask that all rooms be located on one floor or grouped together.

____ Choose one to three local hotels as options for your guests. Determine the type of hotel based on the amenities that your guests will enjoy, i.e. indoor/outdoor pool; variety of nearby dining options; and convenient to get to from the highway and the other planned family activities.

____ If you have more than one hotel option for your guests, choose hotels located in close proximity for convenient carpooling.

____ Provide driving directions to the hotel(s) for your guests.

____ The Hotel Group Sales Consultant will provide a code for your family members to use when making their reservations. The code will represent your block of rooms for your family.

____ Provide hotel(s) information to your family members as soon as possible giving them plenty of time to make reservations.

____ Request a reservations report for your group in order to monitor which guests have made reservations.

HOTEL BOOKING COST COMPARISON

Number of guests _____
Rooms needed _____
Check-in Date _____
Check-out Date _____

Hotel	Phone#/Location	Check In - Out	Cost per night

MEALS/MENU

No family reunion is complete without the traditional meal in the form of a noon luncheon and/or banquet dinner.

While some will have each catered many families insist on doing some of the cooking themselves. In preparation of the big event set aside time to focus on great recipes and traditional meals your family has whipped up and served over the years.

Who can forget when visiting family on some special occasion inquiring about a dish that tasted absolutely fantastic? Whether it was well seasoned pot roast, smoke BBQ ribs or southern fried chicken, we could not resist getting seconds and just had to have the recipe. Many of these very recipes have been in the family for years and passed on from generation to generation.

Preparing for the family reunion is a great time to start collecting recipes in fun and exciting ways. Some planners have sounded the call and gathered all cooks, chefs, bakers and grill masters for a pre-family reunion cook off including the traditional dishes that will be served up at the reunion luncheon.

The cook off would be an ideal time to exchange and record recipes as you taste traditional meals, test newly introduced cuisine and create the family reunion menu.

Organize times and locations for the whole family to come together for meals. Cooking together can be fun and a great time to swap recipes, exchange cooking methods, reveal secret ingredients and tell some hilarious stories while doing so.

Once the family cook-off is had, add the highlights of the day in a family newsletter. Talk about the turn out, meals cooked, recipes shared and taste tests as well as other unforgettable moments of the day.

Your newsletter can be written in such a way as to build anticipation for the family reunion event.

85

Date:	Menu		
Breakfast Time:	Main Course	Drinks	Dessert
Lunch Time:	Main Course	Drinks	Dessert
Dinner Time:	Main Course	Drinks	Dessert

Date:	Menu		
Breakfast Time:	Main Course	Drinks	Dessert
Lunch Time:	Main Course	Drinks	Dessert
Dinner Time:	Main Course	Drinks	Dessert

Date:	Menu		
Breakfast Time:	Main Course	Drinks	Dessert
Lunch Time:	Main Course	Drinks	Dessert
Dinner Time:	Main Course	Drinks	Dessert

Date:	Menu		
Breakfast Time:	Main Course	Drinks	Dessert
Lunch Time:	Main Course	Drinks	Dessert
Dinner Time:	Main Course	Drinks	Dessert

My Family Reunion Recipes

Whether you're having a family cook-off or just
collecting recipes to be passed down to the next generation
this is the place to record them all.

Recipes

Title: _____
Date Recipe was Received: _____
Longevity of Recipe: _____ years _____ generations
Origination: _____
_____

Phone: _____ Mobile: _____
Email: _____ Other: _____

Ingredients:
_____
_____
_____
_____

Process:
_____
_____
_____
_____
_____
_____
_____
_____

Notes:
_____
_____
_____
_____

Recipes

Title: _____
Date Recipe was Received: _____
Longevity of Recipe: _____ years _____ generations
Origination: _____
_____

Phone: _____ Mobile: _____
Email: _____ Other: _____

Ingredients:
_____
_____
_____
_____

Process:
_____
_____
_____
_____
_____
_____
_____

Notes:
_____
_____
_____
_____

Recipes

Title: _____
Date Recipe was Received: _____
Longevity of Recipe: _____ years _____ generations
Origination:_____
_____

Phone: _____ Mobile: _____
Email: _____ Other: _____

Ingredients:
_____
_____
_____
_____

Process:
_____
_____
_____
_____
_____
_____

Notes:
_____
_____
_____
_____

Recipes

Title: _____
Date Recipe was Received: _____
Longevity of Recipe: _____ years _____ generations
Origination:_____
_____

Phone: _____ Mobile: _____
Email: _____ Other: _____

Ingredients:
_____
_____
_____
_____

Process:
_____
_____
_____
_____
_____
_____
_____

Notes:
_____
_____
_____
_____

Recipes

Title: _____
Date Recipe was Received: _____
Longevity of Recipe: _____ years _____ generations
Origination:_____
_____

Phone: _____ Mobile: _____
Email: _____ Other: _____

Ingredients:
_____
_____
_____
_____

Process:
_____
_____
_____
_____
_____
_____
_____

Notes:
_____
_____
_____
_____

Recipes

Title: _____

Date Recipe was Received: _____

Longevity of Recipe: _____ years _____ generations

Origination:_____
_____

Phone: _____ Mobile: _____

Email: _____ Other: _____

Ingredients:
_____
_____
_____
_____

Process:
_____
_____
_____
_____
_____
_____
_____

Notes:
_____
_____
_____
_____

Recipes

Title: _____

Date Recipe was Received: _____

Longevity of Recipe: _____ years _____ generations

Origination: _____
_____

Phone: _____ Mobile: _____

Email: _____ Other: _____

Ingredients:
_____
_____
_____
_____

Process:
_____
_____
_____
_____
_____
_____
_____

Notes:
_____
_____
_____
_____

Recipes

Title: _____
Date Recipe was Received: _____
Longevity of Recipe: _____ years _____ generations
Origination:_____
_____
Phone: _____ Mobile: _____
Email: _____ Other: _____

Ingredients:
_____
_____
_____
_____

Process:
_____
_____
_____
_____
_____
_____

Notes:
_____
_____
_____
_____

Recipes

Title: _____
Date Recipe was Received: _____
Longevity of Recipe: _____ years _____ generations
Origination:_____
_____

Phone: _____ Mobile: _____
Email: _____   Other: _____

Ingredients:
_____
_____
_____
_____

Process:
_____
_____
_____
_____
_____
_____
_____

Notes:
_____
_____
_____
_____

CERTIFICATE AWARDS OF ACHIEVEMENT

Honor family members who reached pinnacles in their life that has enriched your heritage and make you proud of the institution of family.

Recognize the oldest living relative, who is still spry enough to grace the dance floor; the cousin who earned a full four-year scholarship to college; the uncle who just retired from a company he worked at for 35 years; the mother and father who celebrates 50 years of wedlock; or the grandmother who lives to see four generations.

Name	Age	Relation	Accomplishments	Other

You'll find editable, printable certificates, poems, flyers, banners and more in Fimark's Family Reunion Planner software application or go to Fimark Family Reunion Planning resource online at www.family-reunion-planner.fimark.net to download one.

MUSIC

If and when music is selected for any of your planned events, be mindful of respecting the consciences of all your family members. It is likely, that not all will have the same taste in music. Choose music that most can relate to and will enjoy. Arrange for one family member to be in charge of the music. Be mindful of the volume of the music if played in public areas. Older family members may also be sensitive to loud volume. You'll find a great family reunion music list at www.family-reunion-planner.fimark.net.

MUSIC SELECTION SHEET

Artist	Title	Running Time

DIRECTIONS/MAPS

Have on hand copies of driving directions and maps to all locations of events for your out-of-town guests. And even some of your local family members may need to know how to get to the cookout at Aunt Shirley's house.

Directions	Map

You'll find directions and maps and more in Fimark's Family Reunion Planner software application or go to www.family-reunion-planner.fimark.net to download one.

FUND RAISER IDEAS

Create family heirloom using photos of ancestors for auction.

Auction off genealogy research documents.

Auction off award certificates, business ownership, deeds, antiques and Heirlooms.

Write biographies of notable family members and have them printed and bound. - Auction off biographies

Have artist hand paint beautiful colorful 18x24 portrait.
Auction off portrait heirlooms. For portrait services write us at fimarkhome@gmail.com

Video tape the research events from start to finish. – Auction off video

Have custom designed greeting cards covering annual celebratory events of the year with family names inscribed on the cards. Place the cards in a gift basket. Auction off the cards. To order greeting cards write us at fimarkhome@gmail.com

You'll find other great fund raiser ideas at www.family-reunion-planner.fimark.net.

REUNION EVALUATION FORM

(To be completed by Coordinator, Committee Members and Volunteers)

Element	Yes	No	Comments and/or Improvements
Satisfactory number of participants	☐	☐	
Goals achieved	☐	☐	
Stayed within overall budget	☐	☐	
Committee members completed assignments	☐	☐	
Committee members stayed within budget	☐	☐	
Committee Head communicated regularly with members	☐	☐	
Sufficient number of helpers	☐	☐	
Committee met regularly or had sufficient number meetings	☐	☐	
Site location well suited for the event	☐	☐	
Favorable comments received about location	☐	☐	
Parking was adequate	☐	☐	
Amenities were adequate	☐	☐	
Hospitality was adequate (tables, chairs, food, space, on-site personnel, etc.)	☐	☐	
Lunch program was well received	☐	☐	
Equipment was adequate	☐	☐	
Presentation of the food/service was adequate	☐	☐	
Sufficient food, snacks, beverages, refreshments for all	☐	☐	
Sufficient number of mailings/advance notices with/minimum return	☐	☐	
Registration went smoothly & organized	☐	☐	
OTHER:			
Thank You Notes sent to volunteers	☐	☐	

NEXT REUNION PLANS

Date: Location:
Activities:

Date: Location:
Activities:

Date: Location:
Activities:

Date: Location:
Activities:

PEDIGREE CHART

8 Granddad's Father
Born:
Place:
Marr:
Place:
Died:
Place:

4 Grand Father ------

Born:
Place:
Marr: a long time ago
Place:
Died:
Place: someplace around here

9 Granddad's Mother
Born:
Place: someplace around here
Died:
Place:

2 My Father ------

Born:
Place:
Marr:
Place: someplace around here
Died:
Place:

10 Dad's Mother's Dad
Born:
Place:
Marr:
Place:
Died:
Place:

5 Dad's Mother ------

Born: a long time ago
Place:
Died:
Place:

11 Dad's Mother's Mom
Born:
Place: someplace around here
Died:
Place:

1 Me Myself ------

Born:
Place: someplace around here
Marr:
Place:
Died:
Place:

12 Mom's Father's Dad
Born:
Place:
Marr:
Place:
Died:
Place:

6 Mother's Father
Born:
Place:
Marr:
Place:
Died: a long time ago
Place:

13 Mom's Father's Mom
Born:
Place:
Died:
Place: someplace around here

3 My Mother
Born:
Place:
Died:
Place:

14 Mom's Mother's Dad
Born:
Place: someplace around here
Marr:
Place:
Died:
Place:

7 Mom's Mother
Born:
Place:
Died:
Place: someplace around here

15 Mom's Mother's Mom
Born:
Place:
Died:
Place:

FAMILY GROUP WORK SHEET

	No.
Patriarchs Full Name:	**Husband** #_____
Born:	Place:
Married:	Place:	**Wife** #_____
Died:	Place:
Buried at:		**Sources and Notes:**
His Father:		
Born:	Place:	
Died:	Place:	
His Mother:		
Born:	Place:	
Died:	Place:	
Wife's Maiden Name:		
Born:	Place:	
Died:	Place:	
Buried at:	Other Marr:	
Her Father:		
Born:	Place:	
Died:	Place:	
Her Mother:		
Born:	Place:	
Died:	Place:	

M/F	Children: Give names in full in order of birth, living or dead.	Born: Date: Place:	Died: Date: Place:	Married: Spouse: Date: Place:
	1.			
	2.			
	3.			
	4.			
	5.			
	6.			
	7.			
	8.			
	9.			
	10.			

CEMETERY TRANSCRIPTION FORM

Cemetery Location: _____

Gravestone/Tombstone Description	Inscription: (Birth, Death, details)
Headstone: Footstone: Engraved Art: Photography: Grave Decor: Notes:	
Headstone: Footstone: Engraved Art: Photography: Grave Decor: Notes:	
Headstone: Footstone: Engraved Art: Photography: Grave Decor: Notes:	
Headstone: Footstone: Engraved Art: Photography: Grave Decor: Notes:	

For help with the description, documentation and historicity of tombstones consider these resources.

American Antiquarian Society, www.davidrumsey.com/farber

The Association for Gravestone Studies, www.gravestonestudies.org
AGS promotes the study of gravestones from historical and artistic perspectives, expands public awareness of the significance of historic grave markers, and encourages individuals and groups to record and preserve gravestones. At every opportunity, AGS cooperates with groups that have similar interests.

HEIRLOOM POSSESSION VERIFICATION

Date	Artifact and Condition Indicate Manufacturing # Certificates of Authenticity/Ownership, etc.	Possessor (Name, Address, Phone)	Inheritor (Name, Address, Phone)

MILITARY RECORDS RESEARCH CHECKLIST

Name: _____

	Colonial Wars	American Revolution 1775-1783	1784-1811	War of 1812 (1812-1815)	Indian Wars 1815-1858	Patriot War 1838	Mexican War 1846-1848	Civil War 1861-1865 (for Confederates	Service 1866 forward	Spanish-American War 1898-1899	Philippine Insurrection 1899-1902	World War I 1917-1918	World War II 1941-1945
Name													
Birth - Current													
Name													
Birth - Current													
Name													
Birth - Current													
Name													
Birth - Current													
Name													
Birth - Current													
Name													
Birth - Current													

ANCESTRAL RESEARCH WORK SHEET

Full Name _____
First, middle, last, nickname, maiden name

Surname _____

Spelling Variants of Surname _____

Social Security Number _____ _____ _____

Date of Birth _____
If exact date of birth is unknown; give approximate five-year range

Place of Birth _____

Physical Description _____
_____

Marital Status

_____
_____
_____

Name of spouse(s) or ex-spouse(s) and date of marriage(s) and divorces (s), if applicable

Occupations/ Trade/ Business _____

Employers/Partners _____
Include dates and addresses if known

Last Known Address _____

_____
List many as possible. If exact address unknown, list city and/or state. Include dates of former addresses.

_____

_____

_____

Prior Telephone Numbers

( ) _____ _____   ( ) _____ _____   ( ) _____ _____

Education _____
    High school, vocational-technical and college. Include years attended and whether graduated.

Military Service _____
    Branch, rank, dates, place of discharge, serial number

Religion _____

_____

Hobbies _____

Financial Status _____

Children: Names, Birth Dates, Birth Places _____

_____

_____

_____

Name/Address/Telephone of Friends

_____

_____

_____

Name/Address/Telephone of Friends

_____

_____

_____

Name/Address/Telephone of Friends

_____

_____

_____

Name/Address/Telephone of Friends

_____

_____

_____

Name/Address/Telephone of Friends

_____

_____

_____

Name/Address/Telephone of Friends

_____

_____

_____

Name/Address/Telephone of Friends

_____

_____

_____

Name/Address/Telephone of Friends

_____

_____

_____

Family Reunion Event Planning Survey

Legendary Heritage Heirlooms

Hello Family!
We are considering holding a family reunion in the year _____, and need your input. Please give the follow careful consideration and mail/fax or email this form back to us ASAP.

Will you and your household be able to attend the family reunion event?
___Yes ___No ___Don't know

Select the desired reunion duration? ___ 1 afternoon ___ weekend ___long weekend

Choose a desired theme for the event.
1. Traditional   _____
2. Living Legends Ball   _____
3. Family Reunion Luxury Cruise _____
4. Family Reunion Summer Fest   _____
5. Genealogy Homestead Tour   _____

Reunion Location ideas_____

Best time of year_____

Food ideas_____

Activity ideas_____

Additional comments_____

_____

Add names and addresses of families who may be overlooked.

1. _____

2. _____

3. _____

…survey continued.

Please help us keep our records up to date. List first, middle and last names of all family members in your household along with date of birth (DOB).

Head(s) of Household

First Name_____ Middle _____ Last Name_____ DOB _____

First Name_____ Middle _____ Last Name_____ DOB _____

Others

First Name_____ Middle _____ Last Name_____ DOB _____

First Name_____ Middle _____ Last Name_____ DOB _____

First Name_____ Middle _____ Last Name_____ DOB _____

First Name_____ Middle _____ Last Name_____ DOB _____

First Name_____ Middle _____ Last Name_____ DOB _____

Home Address_____

City_____ State_____ Zip code_____

Country_____

Is This a New address?   ___Yes   ___No

Home Phone_____ Cell Phone_____

Email_____

Website_____

What activities and themes do you suggest for future family reunions?

_____

FAMILY REUNION LUNCH AND DINNER PROGRAM

Legendary Heritage Heirlooms

Reception Hall   Location: _____

Live Band: Band(s): _____

Catering: Serving Style: _____

Welcome Speech: Name: _____

Mix Music and Mingle:

"Then and Now" Skits: Name: _____

Poetry Recital: Name: _____

Singing:
    Group and Solo Artists: Name(s): _____

History Recital: Name(s): _____

Honorary Awards: Name(s): _____

Storytelling: Name(s): _____

Music Selection:

After Dinner Dancing: Song: _____
Husbands and Wives: Song: _____
Fathers and Daughter: Song: _____
Mother and Sons: Song: _____
Grand's and Grandchildren: Song: _____
Children: Song: _____
Line Dance: Song: _____

Dessert:

Acknowledgements: Name(s): _____

Closing Words: Name(s): _____

Other: _____

FAMILY REUNION ITINERARY

Legendary Heritage Heirlooms

Theme: _____

Date: _____

Slogan:"_____"

THURSDAY

3:00- 7:00 PM   Registration (room check-in from 4:00 PM)
Family information on interactive display, including activities and games.

5:00-7:00 PM   Come-and-Go supper in suite #_____

7:00-9:00 PM   Welcoming, Orientation, Ice-Breakers

FRIDAY

7:00 AM   Morning Exercise

8:00-11:00 AM   Banquet Breakfast

9:00-11:30 AM   Free time for visiting sports, gaming including, tennis, fishing, golf, hiking, swimming, etc.

12:00 - 2:30 PM   Mini Cruise (Pay at arrival - Adult: $15.00   Child: $9.00

3:00-4:00 PM   Rest Refresh and Visit

4:00 PM   Family Conference, Awards Ceremony.

5:30 PM   Honorary Dinner

7:00 PM   Memoriam, singing, storytelling.

                                                       Continued…

SATURDAY

7:00 AM	Morning Exercise
7:00-8:30 AM	Banquet Breakfast
9:00 AM	Home Stead and City Tour
5:00 PM	Rest Refresh and Visit
5:30 PM	Group Photos in the Park
6:00 PM	Family Dinner
7:30 PM	Family Entertainment Special

SUNDAY

7:00 AM	Morning Exercise
11:00 AM	Brunch & Inspirational Speech
1:30 PM	Video show
2:00 PM	Farewells

THE _____ FAMILY REUNION

"A Legacy of Hope and Love"

February 13, 2014

Greetings Family and Friends!

The members of the _____ Family Reunion Committee are pleased to invite one and all to our 18th Martin Family Reunion at Capital City July 19 - 21, 2014. Fun and exciting activities await all attendees based on the theme, "A legacy of Hope and Love."

We chose the Capital City because it is the city of the _____ homestead and therefore rich with family history. We will be headquartered at the recently renovated Delta Gold Hotel in Capital City, in _____ State just outside of _____. Nearby is the Golden Ring Mall where you can shop until you drop.

Please make your Reunion Hotel Reservation(s) early. The special _____ room rate for 2 double deluxe is $79. _____

The Family is having a Ball! The Living Legends Ball. Join us in the Vineyard Ballroom, Seating - 500 persons. Accommodations will be made according to date of Reunion Registration - not hotel registration. Please get your Reunion Registration in as soon as possible to guarantee seating in the main ballroom.

Hotel information is as follows:
Hotel Name_____
Street Address_____
Room Size_____ Price_____
Phone _____ Web site _____
Register By _____ Accommodation Dates _____

Included in this reunion packet are: General Information
Schedule of Events and Optional Activities
Reunion Registration Form – Deadline is May 2nd
Souvenir Booklet Ad Application - Due April 21st
Scholarship Information - Due June 2nd

Call (contact name) _____ – (phone) _____ for Application Packet.

Sincerely,

Name_____ -- Phone_____
Local and National Registration Chairperson
2014 _____ Family Reunion

Free Evaluation of The Family Reunion Planner Software Application

There are many exciting features to the Family Reunion Planning interface you'll want to know about.

Help Feature (free access in the evaluation version)
There is a new help feature added to assist you when using the Family Reunion Planner interface. Find out how to locate and use applications, tools and templates.

Interface Features (Complete Version Only)
The family reunion planner checklists appear on the blue bar along with printable reunion stationary, invitations, certificates and the keepsake family reunion booklet just above the panels. The planner worksheets, spreadsheets and assignment documents can be retrieved under the "Workbooks" tab.

T-Shirt Designer (Free access)
The T-shirts panel is a fun place to start designing your family reunion t-shirts. Choose several different logos or find logos on the Theme Selector Panel.

Family Reunion Store (Free access)
A new family reunion store was recently added to your interface. Find everything you need from party favors to awards and certificates. Great gift grab bag selection, keepsakes and mementos. Special gifts for the elders of the family.

Download family reunion music. Read excerpts from the most popular reunion planning books and order great outdoor cooking recipe books
Here's a short cut... http://astore.amazon.com/family-reunion-20

Theme Selector (Free access)
Use the Theme Selector to choose from five popular reunion themes for your event along with pre-written theme related activities, itinerary and luncheon/banquet dinner programs. Each theme has it's own invitations, greeting cards, flyer stationary and matching t-shirt, apron and cap combo ready to order.

Timeline Planner (Complete Version Only)
Use the timeline planner for daily planning reminders and alerts to special reunion supply buying seasons.

Keepsake Family Reunion Booklet (Complete Version Only)
Includes an updated Keepsake Family Reunion Booklet complete with instructions.

Access the Family Reunion Planner evaluation version at
http://family-reunion planner.fimark.net/step1.html
and use this books ISBN number to log in.

Purchase the full version at http://family-reunion planner.fimark.net

Get Family Reunion Website Builder Reviews and Recommendations.

Find out how to build your own family reunion website and start taking event fee payments, add your event photos, write family history, add a blog and guest book and make a family tree.

Members can RSVP online and you can send email blasts to everyone in your contact database right from your website. Get more information at
http://family-reunion-planner.fimark.net/familyreunionwebsite.html

References

American Antiquarian Society, www.davidrumsey.com/farber/

Association for Gravestone Studies, www.gravestonestudies.org/

Thomas, Willa J. "May: Family Reunion Month." Reference Services Review 14, 3 (Fall 1986): 64-67

Wikipedia, Keyword: "Family Reunions"
http://en.wikipedia.org/wiki/Family_reunion

Resources

Event Planning
www.family-reunion.com
www.familyreunion.com

Family Reunion Planning News
http://familyreunionplanners.blogspot.com
http://groups.yahoo.com/group/family-reunion-planning
www.reunionsmag.com

Family Reunion Planning Tips
http://familyreunionplanners.blogspot.com
www.family-reunion-planner.fimark.net

Invitational Printables
www.family-reunion-planner.fimark.net

Genealogy
www.reunions.afrigeneas.com
www.cyndislist.com/reunions.htm

Software
http://familyreunionplanners.blogspot.com

Recipes
www.bigelowteablog.com/tag/family-reunion-month

Supplies
http://astore.amazon.com/family-reunion-20

T-shirts
www.customink.com
www.zazzle.com/zzibcnet

Index

acknowledgements, 5
activities, 7, 8, 78, 80
activities worksheet, 78
advanced timeline planner, 15
agenda, 86
agenda for lunch/dinner program, 86
ancestral, 114
ancestral research work sheet, 114
application, 124
assignments, 69
assignments worksheets, 68
ball, 36
boomers, 4
cemetery transcription form, 110
certificates, 100
checklist, 17
committees, 12, 68
committees lists, 68
consideration element, 76
coordinators, 10
cruise planner, 20
cruises, 20
culture, 31
culture fest, 31
dept. assignments 69
departments list 68
details page, 3
dinner, 86, 119
directions, 102
directions/map worksheet, 102
DNA test, 31
elders, 4
evaluation, 104
event planner worksheet, 73
family culture, 31
family group worksheet, 108
fest, 31
forward, 4
fund raiser ideas, 103
fund raisers, 102
games, 79
genealogy, 33
heirloom, 110
heirloom possession verification, 111
homestead, 34
homestead tour, 34
hotel accommodations checklist, 83

hotel booking cost comparison, 84
hotels, 83, 84
invitation, 122
invitational letter, 122
itinerary, 120
journal, 38
legends ball, 35
living legends ball, 36
lunch, 86, 119
luncheon/dinner program, 119
map, 102
map worksheet, 102
meals, 85, 86
menu, 85, 86
milestones, 4
military, 112
military records research checklist, 112
music selection sheet, 101
my reunion journal, 38
my reunion recipes, 91
needs, 82
needs list, 82
next reunion event plans, 105
notes, 70
observances, 6
overview, 7
pedigree, 106
possible locations, 8, 9
proclamations, 6
references, 125
reunion evaluation sheet, 104
reunion planning 10, 12
reunion planning checklist, 17
scheduling worksheet, 75
site location sheet, 74
software, 124
software evaluation features, 124
survey, 117
survey form letter, 117
thanks, 5
themed planners, 19
themes, 19
timeline, 15
timeline planner, 15
tour, 34
tutorial, 7
worksheets, 7, 69, 73 - 75, 78, 101, 104, 108

Notes

"Year after year

generation after generation

if only for a brief moment

by one path or another

we all here today

and those laid to rest

have found the way back home. "

"Finding Our Way Back Home"

Written by Mark Askew

Made in the USA
Monee, IL
20 May 2021